vivian varney guyler
instructor in art history, temple university
tyler school of art
philadelphia, pennsylvania

design in nature

published by art resource publications | f. louis hoover, *editor*

a division of davis publications, inc.
worcester, massachusetts

To Anne, Amanda, Carleton and Sam

Copyright 1970
Davis Publications, Inc.
Worcester, Massachusetts

Library of Congress catalogue card number: 76-93119

SBN number: 87192-031-X

Printing: Davis Press, Inc.

Type: Melior Italic

Design: Panagiota Darras

Photos: the author

Second printing 1971

introduction

Nature can play an important role in the teaching of art and the preparation of young artists. It can help them develop an awareness of the visual properties of shape, line, color, value, texture and space. It is often through nature that our earliest ideas and understanding of these elements are acquired.

This book has been planned to serve as source material for both teachers and students of art. A series of photographs have been selected to define and examine the visual elements as they may be observed in nature. A chapter has been devoted to each of the elements: shape, line, texture, value and space. Each has been examined for its own inherent qualities as well as for its relationship to other elements.

The photographs should serve as an aid in teaching both two- and three-dimensional design by illustrating how the visual content of design (the elements) are found in nature. A student who learns to recognize their presence in nature should be able to see and be aware of them in all visual phenomena, including the visual arts. As a result, he will be better able to create more meaningful imagery of his own.

Nature may also become both an inspiration and a source for his own work. The teacher will see many opportunities to expand upon certain aspects of design which are illustrated in the photographs as he plans activities and projects throughout the year.

It should be kept in mind that the natural objects and areas illustrated in this book are seen through the eye of a camera as controlled by a photographer. Therefore what is seen is not the natural world directly but the natural world through one of the visual art forms — photography. The photographic presentation, although informative and organized to explain and define the design elements, was also undertaken to show natural subject matter selected, organized and interpreted for aesthetic reasons. Photography in each case was regarded as an art form and not merely a means of illustration. The teacher may wish to use the photographs in this regard. He may also choose to show, through the photographic medium, how a certain amount of selection, organization and interpretation distinguishes art from nature, or how an artist may awaken both a greater interest and a greater realization of the natural world through his personal vision.

Because of certain limitations, the element of color could not be used. Color values are discussed in terms of their characteristics and illustrated by blacks, whites and various shades of gray.

V. V.G.

contents

shape *is area* defined. *It may be two-dimensional having length and width but no depth and be called a pattern, or it may be three-dimensional* with length, width and depth or volume, and be called a mass or form.

Shapes in nature are often divided categorically into geometric and non-geometric shapes.

Examples of geometric shapes are the cube and the square, the cylinder, the cone and the oval. The contours of these are more regular than non-geometric shapes. Geometric shapes may be seen in nature with both the microscope and the naked eye.

The round shape of these anthills is another familiar geometric shape.

The hen's egg is one of the most common geometric shapes found in nature.

A violent subterranean disturbance of volcanic origin on the northern coast of Ireland created one of the natural wonders of the world. It is called the Giant's Causeway and is a series of superimposed hexagonal and pentagonal prismatic shapes. These would also be classified as geometric shapes.

The bee's honeycomb is another series of geometric shapes. Its structure of wax contains rows of hexagonal cells formed for the reception of honey and pollen and the bees' eggs.

Non-geometric shapes are more common in nature than geometric shapes. Their contours are irregular and often composed of curved lines.

The impressions made in sand by a human foot are an illustration of shapes that are non-geometric; their contours are irregular and curved.

Peppers are one of a number of vegetables and fruits having non-geometric shapes. Although similar in character, no two have exactly the same dimensions, each pepper possessing an irregular, curved contour.

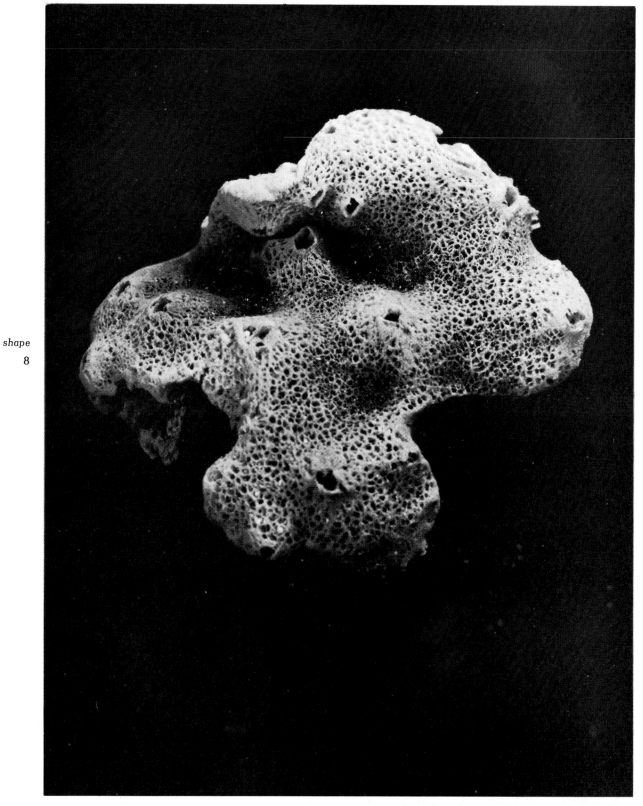

Shapes may be similar in character although composed of different materials. This is true of the sponge and the shape formed by the clouds in front of a setting sun. Both shapes are composed of curved, irregular lines and are non-geometric.

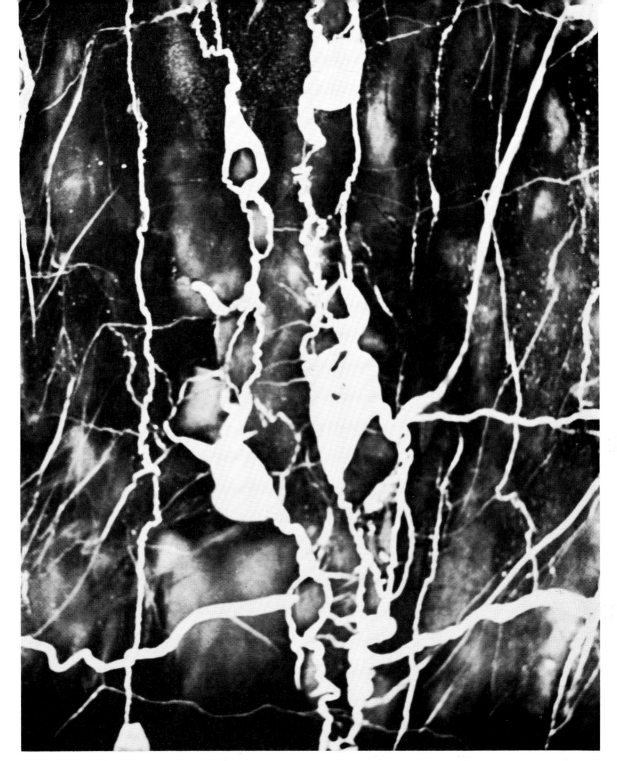

Sometimes it is difficult to distinguish one element of design from another. This may be true in trying to separate shape from line. A line may often be called a shape and a shape may be called a line. A distinction is sometimes made on the basis of degree, a line being identified as that which is longer than it is wide.

These string beans, because of their long, thin shapes, may be called lines.

The difficulty in making a distinction between line and shape may be seen by examining the grain pattern of this marble. The thin white lines become thick and lose their linear character by becoming more heavily concentrated in larger areas. These larger areas of white one would commonly call shapes, but it is often difficult to say at what point a shape becomes a shape and may no longer be called a line.

Shapes may be created in several ways.

A series of superimposed lines may create shapes, as with the small streams of running water.

A shape may be created by a line which sets off a certain area. The line acts as an edge or outline of the shape. This may be seen in the center of the peacock feather.

In nature a series of small shapes sometimes combine to create another shape. The small shapes may be similar and occur in a certain order, sequence or pattern. This order, sequence or pattern is often called the rhythm or rhythmic pattern of the object.

This pine cone is made up of a number of pods or smaller shapes which are arranged in a certain rhythmic pattern. This rhythmic pattern helps identify the object.

The large shape of the rose is composed of a number of smaller shapes: petals arranged in a unique rhythmic pattern.

shape

14

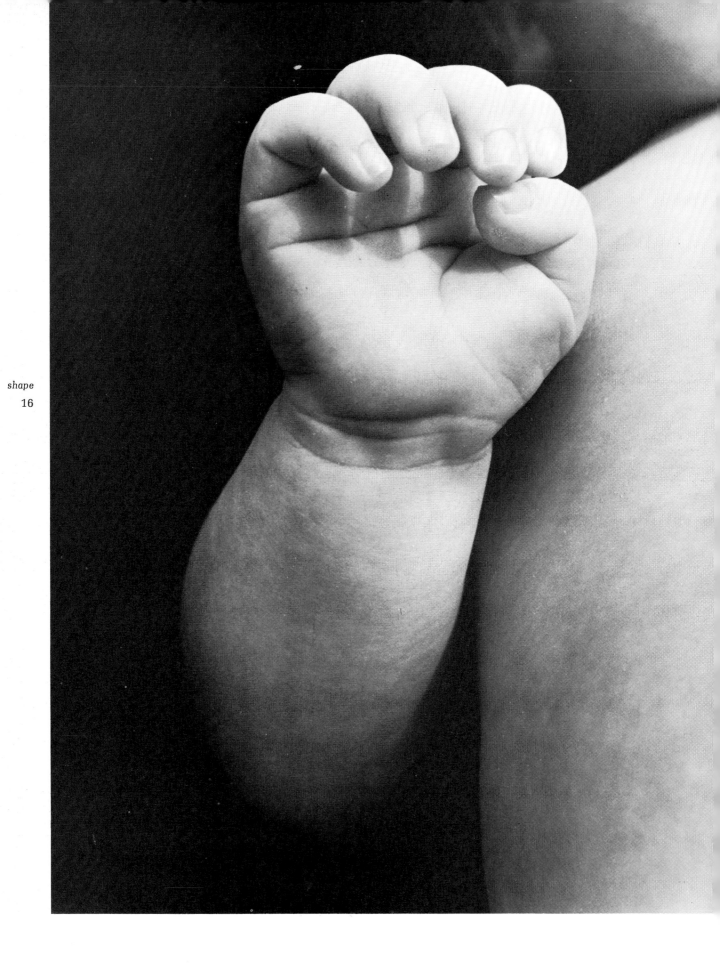

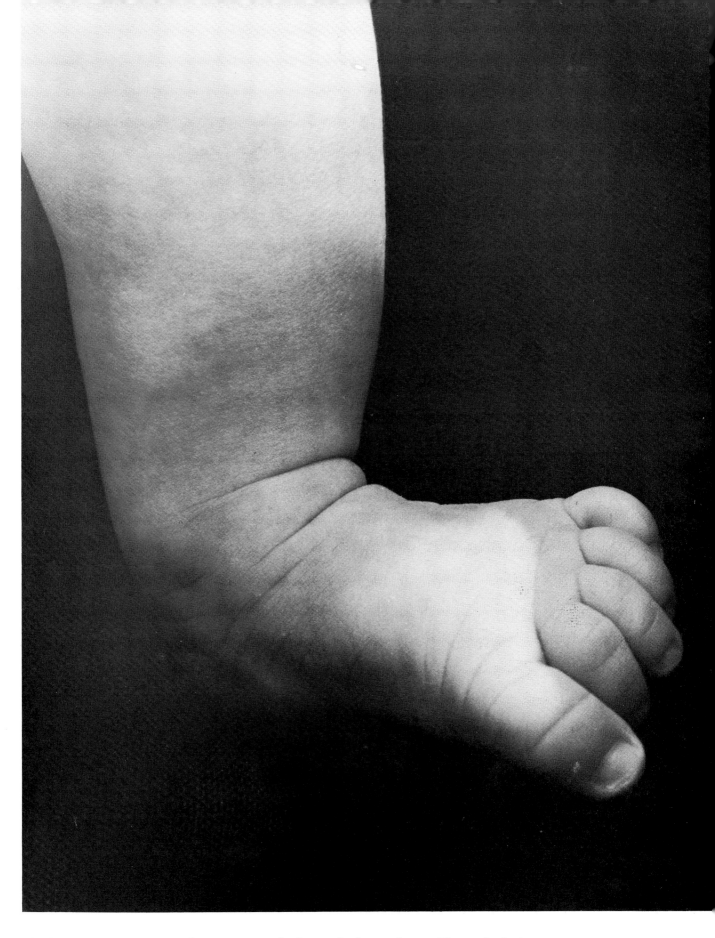

The hand and the foot are shapes composed of other shapes arranged in a rhythmic pattern. The smaller shapes of fingers and toes help to identify the larger shapes. Thus a rhythmic pattern or arrangement of the smaller shapes is an inherent part of the object and helps us to identify it.

Shapes which are alike or similar are often found together in nature. This occurs in animal, vegetable and mineral worlds. Ivy growing over buildings is a familiar example.

It is common, as with this herd of cows, to find a group of the same animals together. Both in body form and in patterning on their hides, they may be said to have similar shapes.

Barnacles attach themselves to marine rocks in a group.

Certain types of flowers grow clustered in groups on a single stock.

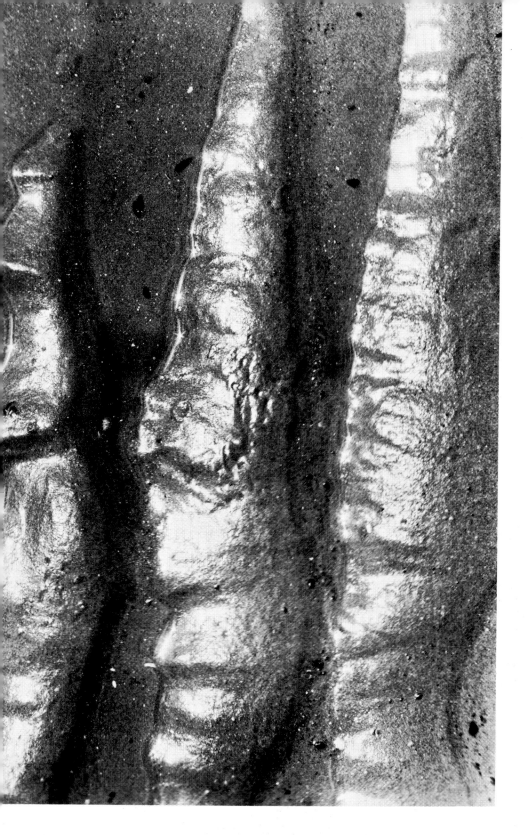

The same natural phenomenon, as the force of tidal
waters, may create many groups of shapes, each
group different in character.

These two groups of sand patterns were found in
different areas along the same shore line.

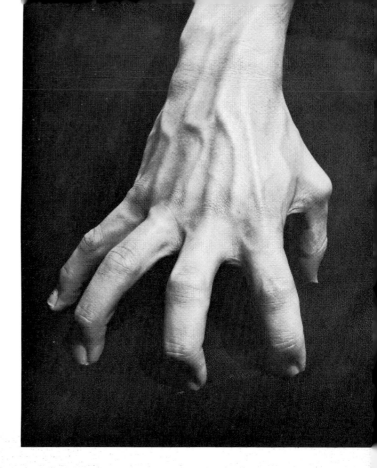

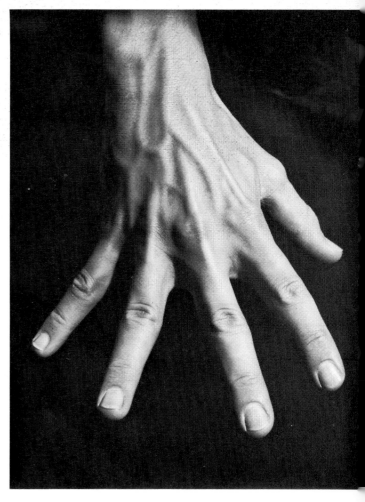

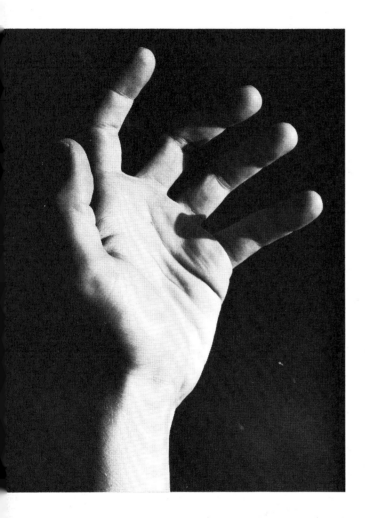

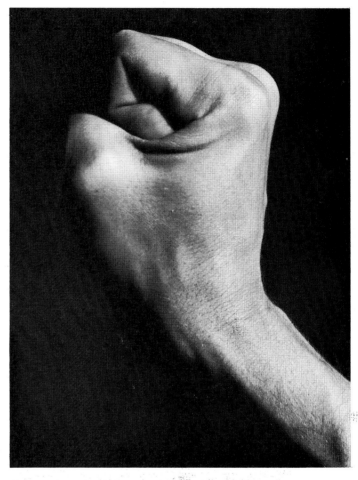

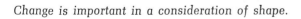

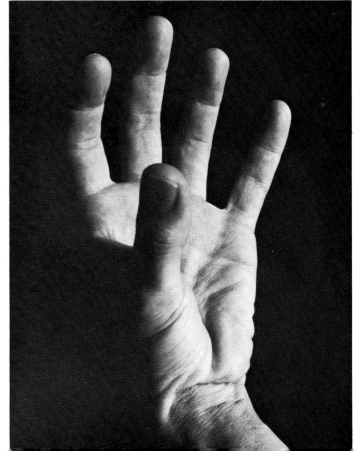

Change is important in a consideration of shape.

Shapes change as a result of growth or movement brought about by forces both external to or inherent in an object or organism.

The man's hand has assumed essentially six different shapes because of movement controlled from within the organism.

shape
26

Position or perspective of the viewer is important in a consideration of change in shape. One object may appear to have many shapes dependent on the angle from which it is seen.

This is the same rock photographed in various positions and from different sides. In a sense, the rock may be said to have six different shapes.

The shape of objects may appear to change when seen in different light, in a different atmosphere, or in a different physical setting.

Under certain lighting conditions and in certain atmospheres, shapes may be revealed in varying degrees from distinct and sharply outlined to completely lost. The color and value of the surrounding objects or background, as well as the viewer's perspective, also affect the shape of objects.

shape
28

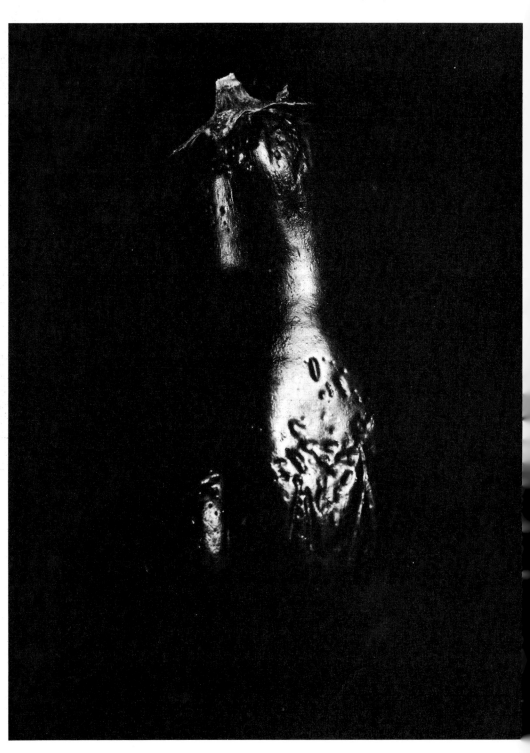

This eggplant loses its shape when seen against a
black background which in color and value is similar to its own. Against a white background, however, the shape is distinctly revealed. The white
contrasts in color and in value with the eggplant's
own color and value.

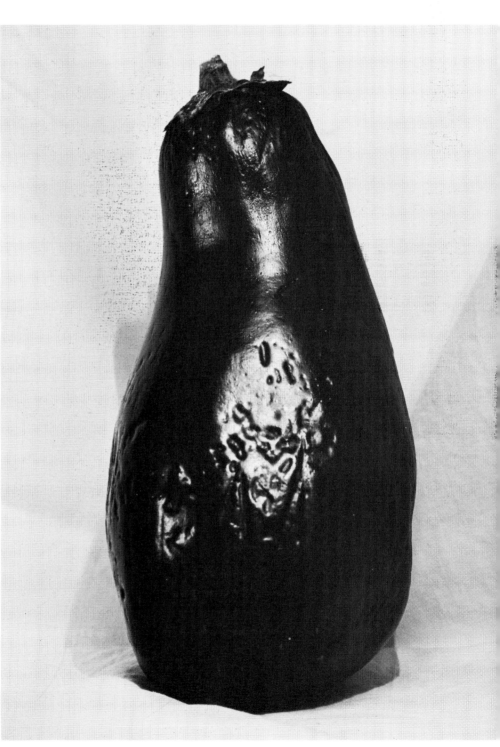

Different parts or layers of an object reveal different shapes. One part or layer may hide another. When seen from the outside, this head of cabbage appears as an essentially round, solid shape.

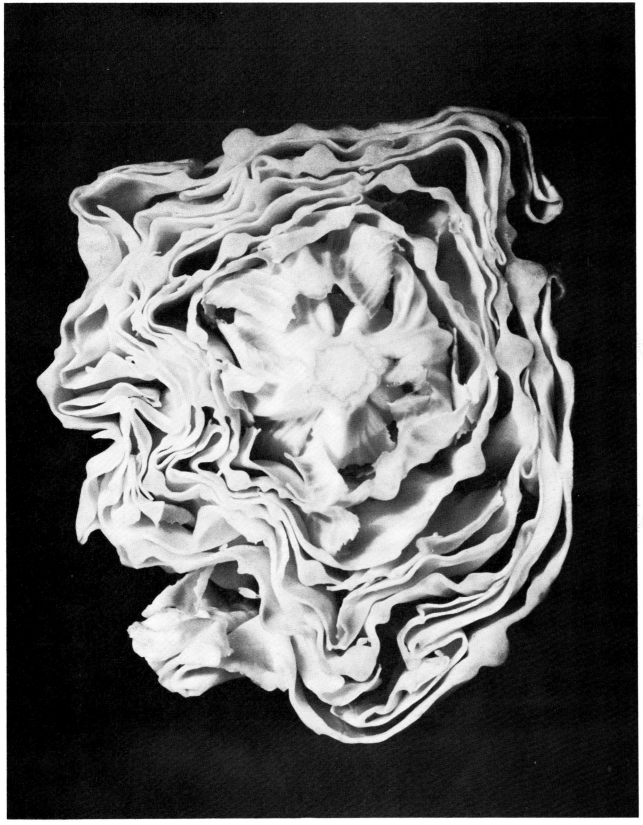

When cut open, however, the same cabbage loses
its round shape. One becomes aware of a number
of superimposed curved lines, shapes or layers
which have been revealed.

line is mark or
mass usually longer than it is wide.
In nature it occurs alone and
in combination with other lines.
All have distinct properties.

Trees and their reflection in a swamp.

One of the properties of line is measure. Measure refers to the dimensions of line, — their length and breadth. Some lines are short, others long; some are thin, others thick.

Trees illustrate the variety of measure of line possible in one object. Some branches are thin, others thick, some short, others long. In winter, the ice and snow changes the measure of the branches by adding material to them.

Other properties of line are type and direction. Both of these properties depend on the nature of the object. This includes its organic structure and components, as well as a number of forces from without such as climate and surroundings. Type of line is described by such terms as straight, curved and zigzag.

The lines formed as a result of the weathering of this piece of wood are curved. With curved lines, directions change.

The lines of these birch trees are essentially straight. Their direction is basically vertical.

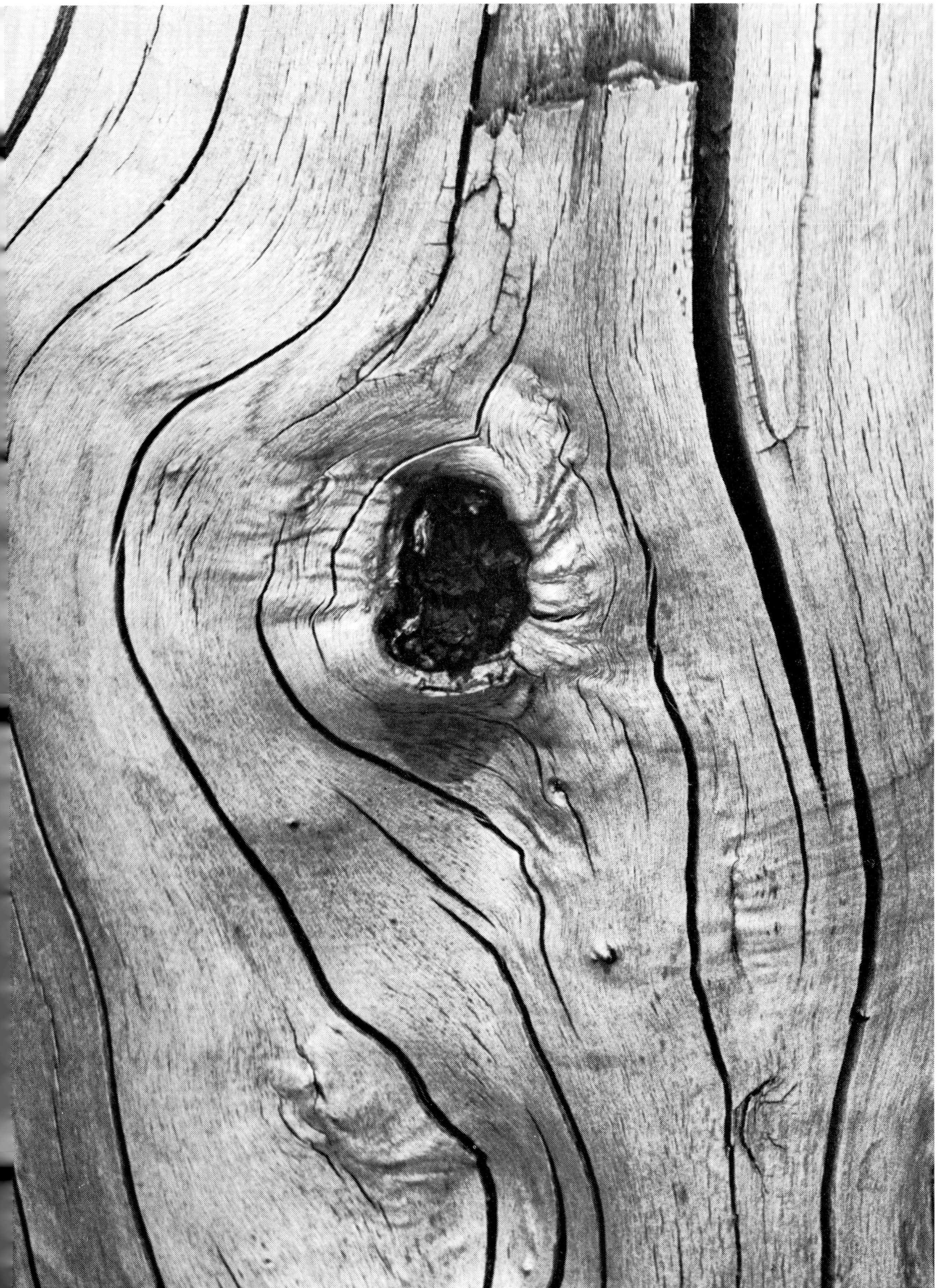

line

37

Some lines in this piece of dried cut wood are cir-
cular, others are straight and jagged. Their directions radiate around and from a central core.

The lines of these weeds are essentially straight, but due to the force of the wind, their dominant direction is diagonal.

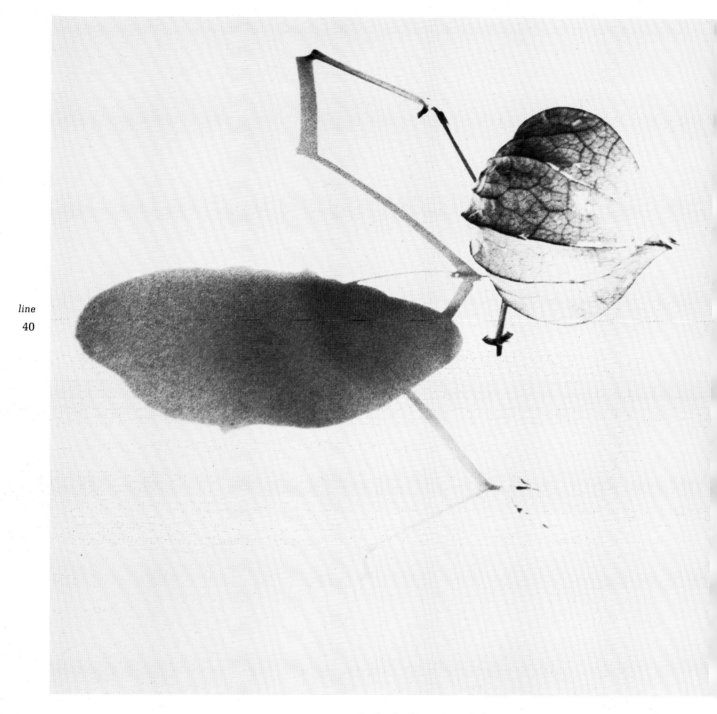

In both the stem of the Japanese lantern and its shadow, and in the twig with its thorns, the line is zigzag.

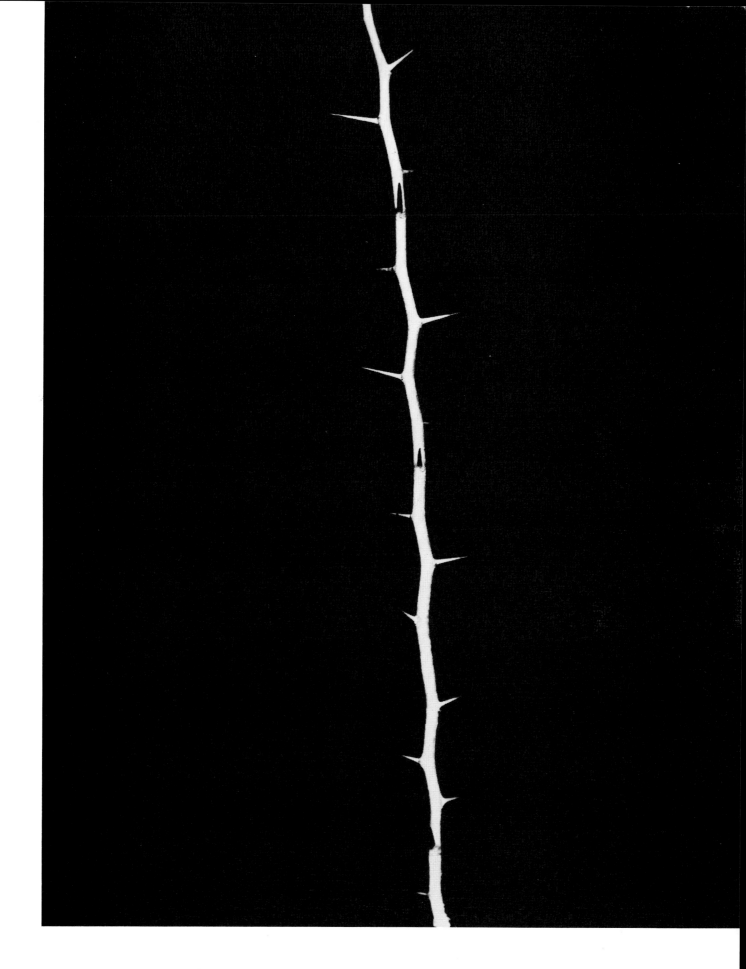

Position of the viewer is important in determining direction of line.

This wheat, bent by the forces of wind and weather, appears to have a backward to forward direction because of the viewer's perspective.

Due partially to the viewer's perspective and partially to the deers' positions, a play of forward and backward line directions is seen here. The line of both their heads and bodies may be said to move either sideward, backward or forward, depending on position and perspective.

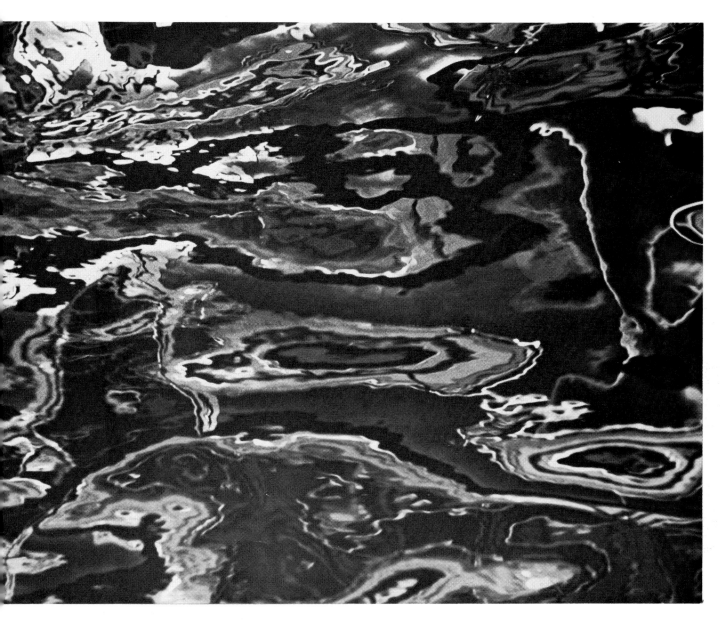

Line in nature may serve many purposes.
It is often an edge and therefore both creates and
defines shapes. As the type of line changes, so does
the character of the shape.

Both of these patterns were created as a result of oil slick on water. The type of line in the above photograph is curved and flowing whereas the type of line in the opposite photograph is jagged. The character of the shapes resulting from these lines is very different as is the effect of the overall design.

Lines create rhythmic patterns.
Repetition of a certain type and direction of line alone or in combination with other types and directions of line creates rhythmic patterns. In nature there is an infinite variety of them.

A distinct rhythmic pattern has been created by the blades of grass. The type as well as the direction of the lines determines the character of the rhythmic pattern.

The rhythmic pattern set up by the repetition of line in this palm leaf is quite distinct from that set up by the blades of grass. The type as well as the direction of line is different.

A sense of space has been created here because the lines of the weeds are superimposed, some placed behind or in front of others. Those lines in back are partially hidden by the lines in front. The lines in back are also less distinct than those in front.

Lines placed in certain ways relative to one's perspective create a sense of space.

The fact that the lines of the more distant cypress trees are narrower, relatively higher and closer to the horizon than those in the foreground, convinces one that space is involved.

Lines may create texture.
Two-dimensional pattern or visual texture often consists of a number of lines. These lines may suggest a texture quite different from the actual or tactile texture of an object: that texture which one experiences when he touches its surface.

In this shell the smooth and regular patterning of line, or the shell's visual texture, suggests smoothness.

The actual texture of these watermelons is smooth. However, the two-dimensional pattern or visual texture created by a combination of lines with ragged edges, suggests a degree of roughness.

Line may change from a two-dimensional to a three-dimensional character due to the weathering process. In doing so, line which once created only two-dimensional pattern or visual texture may create tactile or actual texture.

The wood grain in this photograph is still only two-dimensional. The board itself is relatively smooth. The wood grain in the weathered pier post at right, however, is three-dimensional and creates a tactile or actual texture. Time and conditions have caused the original, smooth post to become rough.

texture *is the characteristic of the surface of an object or area. It may be only two-dimensional and be called a pattern or visual texture. It may be the actual structure of the surface which one experiences when he touches it.*

Bird's nest.

There are many categories in which certain types of texture may be grouped. The two broadest of these are visual texture and tactile or actual texture.

Visual texture is two-dimensional pattern. Certain combinations of lines and shapes with varying values create patterns which suggest various textures. The tactile or actual texture of the same object may be quite different. It is three-dimensional and represents the texture one experiences when he feels the surface of an object.

The visual texture of this rock may be described as rough and uneven because of the pattern of lines and shapes. The actual texture is smooth and hard.

The visual texture of these two apples is quite different. The patterning on the apple at the left suggests a rough surface. The patterning of the apple at the right suggests a much smoother surface. The actual texture of both apples however is the same: smooth.

The tactile or actual texture of an object or area
is dependent partially on the nature and quality of
the material from which it is composed.

The feathers of this duck are smooth and soft.   The shell of this crab is rough and hard.

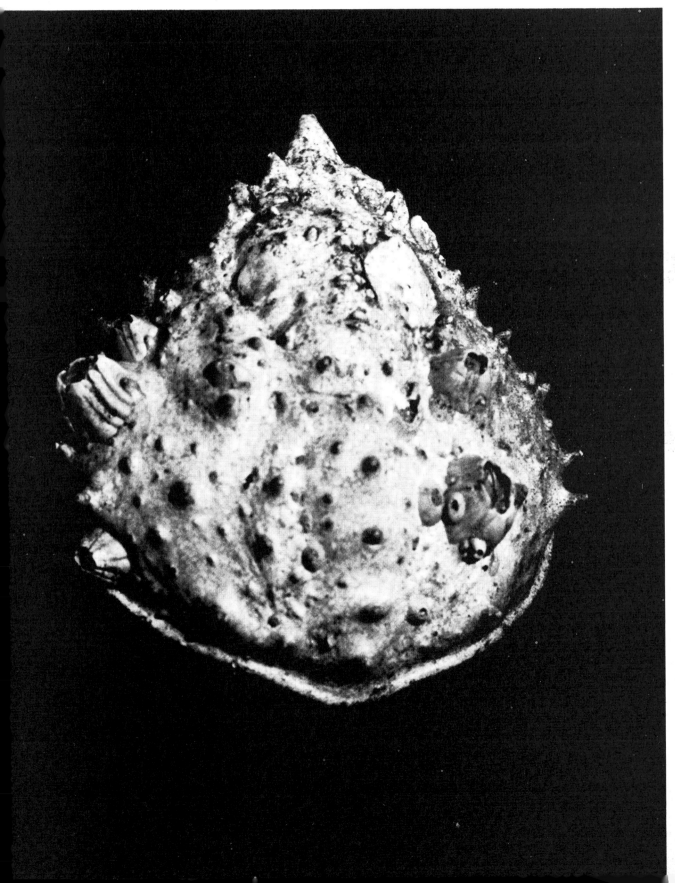

Certain tactile textural qualities such as smoothness or roughness may be shared by a variety of objects although their materials are very different.

This sheep's fleece is rough and soft; the gravel is rough and hard.

The surface of the icicles is smooth and hard. The surface of the melting snow below is smooth and soft.

Objects of the same material may present an entirely different texture. In nature a common example of this is the bark of trees.

The bark of a young maple tree.

The bark of a 200-year old elm.

One object may have a number of different textures; the interior and exterior textures may also be different.

This grapefruit may be said to have at least two textures: relatively smooth and dry on the exterior, smooth and slick on the interior.

One's idea of the texture of objects is affected by the way in which he sees them. The quantity as well as the placement and arrangement of objects affects one's response to them. At certain times their texture may take on a character quite different from their actual texture.

Separately, these stems are smooth in texture. In this scattered arrangement, however, because of the variety of sizes, lengths and directions, they seem to take on a brittle texture.

These weeds, in a seemingly disorganized arrangement, appear lacelike in textural quality. A single plant would not appear to have the same lacelike quality.

That one sees texture differently when objects are alone and when they are grouped is evidenced here by comparing a single thistle and a group of this- tles. Alone, with a white background, one may distinguish the various parts of the plant—the vari- ous textures.

When seen together in a field, the eye finds it dif- ficult to focus on the plants individually. It sees the textural effect or texture of the group, which appears rough and splintery.

Lighting conditions strongly affect the apparent textures of objects.

Various parts of the same object may appear to have different textures because of their position relative to the light sources. This may be illustrated with sections of a head of leaf lettuce.

This section of the lettuce was less directly exposed to the sunlight. In both visual and tactile textures it appears to be lettuce. The patterning and smooth shiny surface are evident.

71

This section was bathed in direct sunlight. Neither in its visual nor in its tactile texture does the substance seem like lettuce. One sees little of the distinguishing patterning of the leaves, nor is the smooth shiny surface evident. The light has also made the lettuce seem softer and lighter in texture.

Objects lighter in value appear softer in actual texture, although they may be harder than objects darker in value.

The coral stone, because of its light value, appears much softer in actual texture than does the pineapple at right where darker values are present. Actually, the tactile texture of the coral stone is much harder.

Texture is affected by differences in the opaqueness, transparency or translucency of a material. It is also influenced by the amount, type, direction and depth reached by the light projected through the material, as well as the degree and type of light reflected from it.

The starfish photographed in relatively shallow water and in strong sunlight have not lost their rough and scaly texture. In an area near the lower right corner, however, because of the sun's direction and reflection, a somewhat hazy visual texture is seen.

A group of rocks photographed in deeper water are almost indistinguishable. The visual texture created because of the direction of the light, the depth of the water and the reflection of the light from the water, is hazy in appearance. This haze conceals the tactile as well as the visual texture of the rocks below.

Age and growth as well as climatic and chemical changes affect both the visual and the tactile textures of objects. The textures of some objects change completely under certain conditions.

Change in textures accompanies every change of season.

A comparison of the same scene in fall and in winter will show how textural change has occurred.

Effects of age, growth and chemical change on textural quality are often seen in the animal and vegetable worlds.

The texture of this potato changed considerably
after two months of exposure to sun and air.

Change in texture due to growth and maturation may be seen by contrasting young and harvested corn.

The texture of the harvested corn is dry and brittle; the once linear visual texture is now three-dimensional.

The texture of the leaves and stalk of the young corn is smooth and glossy. A visual texture consisting of a linear pattern is seen.

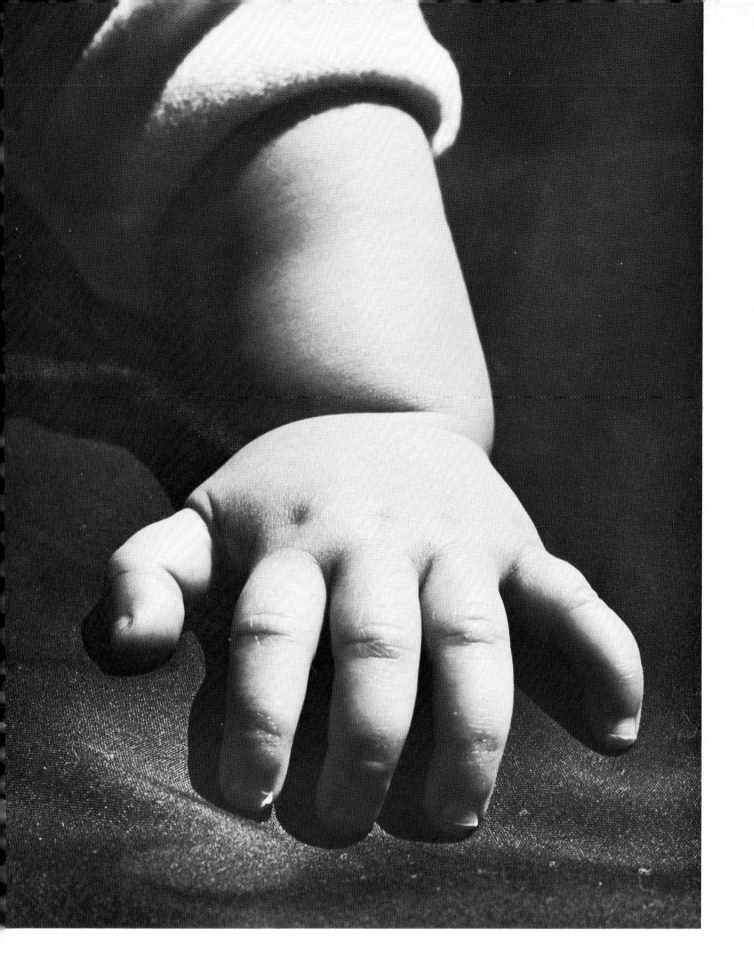

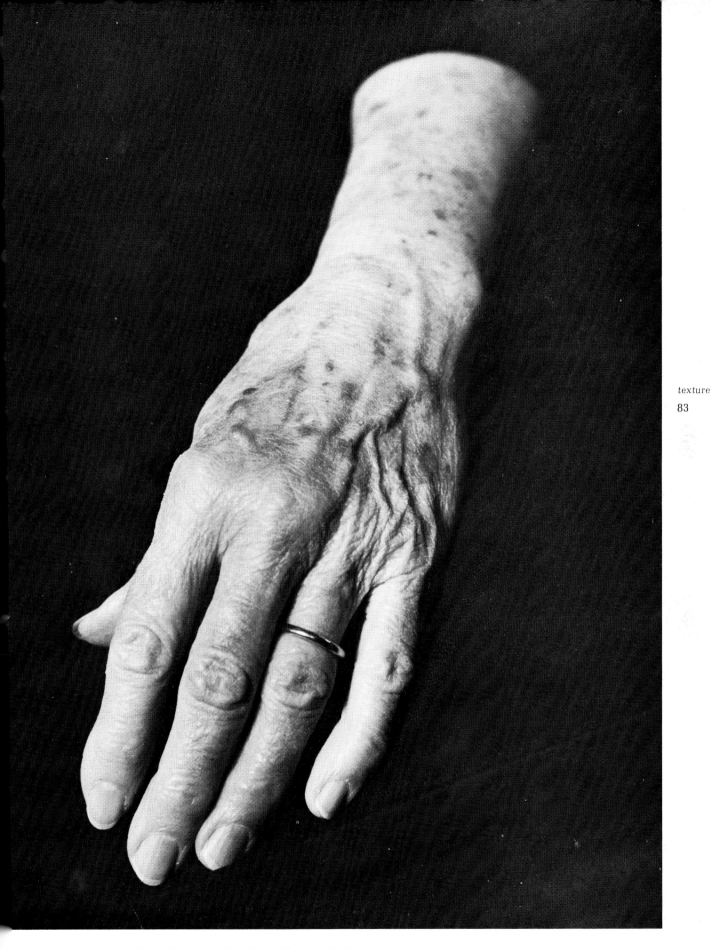

Age also affects the textural quality of human flesh.

value refers

to the lightness or darkness of a color. Each color has a range of values from light to dark which in nature relates to physical laws. In black and white photography, the various values of colors are seen as blacks, whites and grays.

A mushroom.

As one sees them, values are determined by a number of factors and relationships. The type, the amount, and the source of light are important. In addition, the shape, size, composition, color, texture and direction of the objects themselves help determine how one sees value. The properties of surrounding objects and space are also important. Light reveals volume. Volume is three-dimensional mass. Light defines the volume of an object by a change in value. The type of surface and characteristics of the shape are also important to the type of value change.

Values from white to black define the volume of the above shell. The change in value is gradual because of the shape and smoothness of the surface.

Values from white to black also define the volume of the shell at right. Changes in value, however, are often abrupt because of the rough and uneven textural surface.

A sharp direct single source of light often distorts shapes and makes sharper contrasts and fewer values. Some parts of objects or areas may be hidden or made less clear if little or no light reaches them.

The source of light on these shells is coming from the left. Their right sides are often hidden or in shadow as little or no light reaches them.

Certain materials and surfaces reflect light at various angles from the observer's point of view. The introduction of this light creates sharp contrasts and effects the values of the surrounding objects and areas.

An area of sharp value contrast has been created on the surface of this water by the reflection of the sun.

value
90

Strong contrasts, fewer values and less or no detail are seen when objects are lighted from behind. The image against the light appears darker and is often called a silhouette.

The branches and leaves of this tree are seen against bright sunlight. Details, as well as the shape of the branches, are not visible. There are few values and sharp value contrasts. The tree may be said to be silhouetted against the sky.

The bird flying in the path of the sun appears only as a silhouette. It is one dark value only and no detail is seen.

Each color of the spectrum exhibits a number of values from light to dark. The value of the color depends on its relative capacity to absorb and reflect light energy. Darker values of a color absorb more light energy while lighter values reflect more. The same color may have a number of different values. In black and white photography the various values of a color are recorded as blacks, whites and grays.

A pinto bean is made up of two values of brown: dark and light. In black and white photography the darker value of brown in the various shapes is recorded as dark gray; the lighter background is recorded as a lighter gray.

Different colors may have values which are closer than two values of the same color.

The sky and the sea in this photograph are both blue but widely separated in value, as registered in black and white photography, by light and dark gray. The value of blue in the sky is closer to the value of yellow in the sand, although the colors are different.

value

92

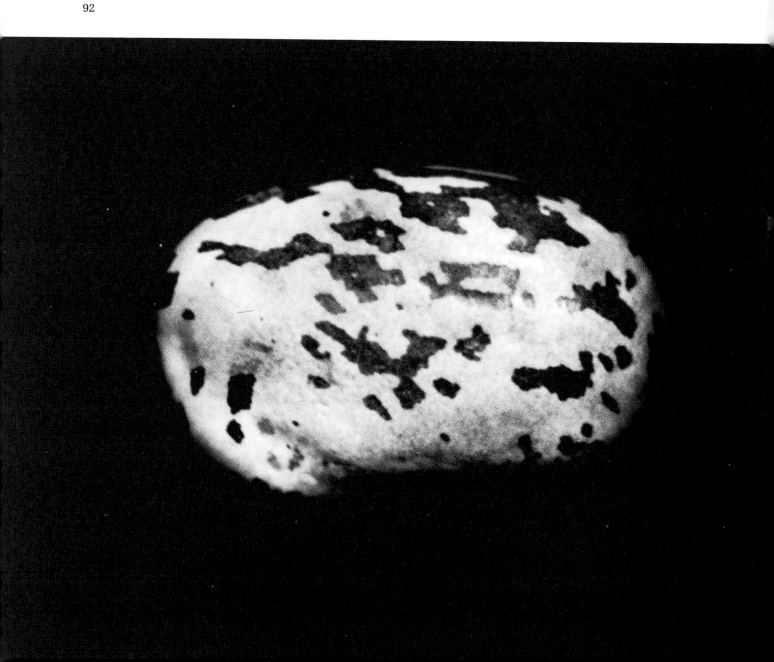

The sharpest value contrast in color exists between black and white. Other value contrasts, while often great, are less sharp.

Strong value contrasts are seen in the head of the zebra with his black and white stripes. The value contrast between the brown and white stripes of the goat's head is not as sharp.

Nature protects certain of her life by the similarity of an organism in color and value to the colors and values in its habitat.

Although it cannot be seen in a black and white photograph, the green, white and yellow of this caterpiller are found in the vegetation surrounding it.

In nature, contrast in color and value helps determine how one sees. An object is easier to distinguish if the area surrounding it is a different color or value.

This black spider is easily defined because it was photographed in a white sink.

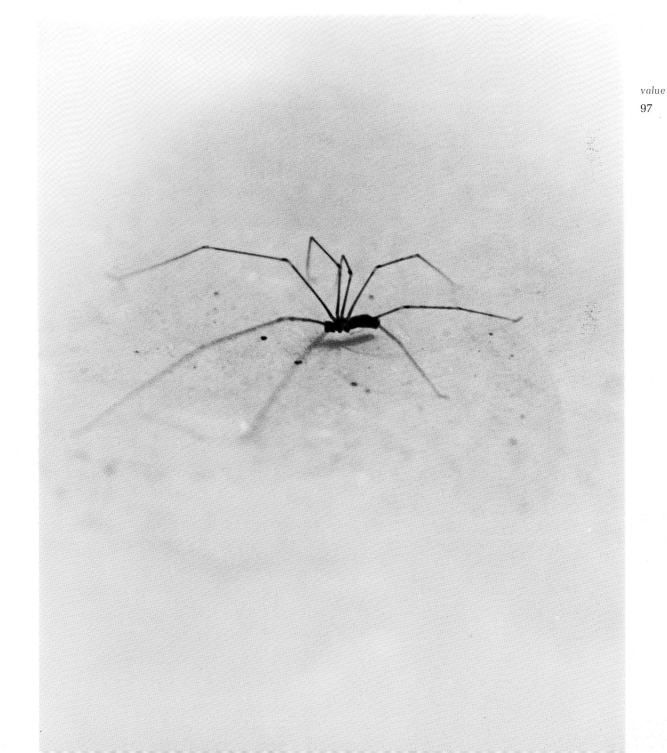

The amount and distribution of the material determines the various values.

Values of objects change when they are seen through another material. The values one sees are determined by the color as well as the degree of opaqueness, transparency or translucency of both the object seen and the material through which it is seen. The amount, type and direction of the light projected and reflected and the depth of the object help determine the values.

In the pattern of frost on the sunlit window above, the change in value is determined by the thickness and distribution of the frost.

The values of the seaweed at right, photographed through water, are determined by all these factors.

The character of shadows relates directly to values. Shadows are created when objects intercept light. The values of such shadows are dependent upon the type of light source and its location, the size, shape and position of the object casting the shadow and the characteristics of the form or area onto which they fall. Shadows of differing values possess different characteristics: some may appear empty or opaque while others are luminous or mysterious.

Shadows cast by the blades of beach grass (somewhat magnified in photo at right) show a gradual change in value due to the relative positions of the blades. The darker shadows near the bottom of the photo are cast by the blades closest to the sand; the lighter shadows (top of photo) are cast by blades farther away from the sand.

The photograph below illustrates two types of shadows: those cast by the pigeons close to the ground are dark and opaque; shadows cast by the trees (not shown) more distant from the ground are lighter in value and more luminous.

value
100

Change in value provides one with information about location in space. This may or may not relate to shadows.

Here position in space is defined partially by the change in value caused by shadows. The ferns and parts of fern closer to the light source are casting shadows on those parts farther away. The more distant the ferns are from the light source, the greater the opportunity for casting shadows. The ferns farthest away are more likely to be darker in value.

In nature values change with increasing distance. Foreground areas and objects, as seen by the edge of this sandy beach, are clearer and show greater value contrast. More distant objects and areas, as the beach and the trees beyond, are ill-defined and show little value contrast.

space *is area or distance between certain points and may be two-, three-, or four-dimensional. Two-dimensional space has length and breadth; three-dimensional has length, breadth, and depth. Four-dimensional space is space-time, or space combining time, motion and three-dimensional space.*

There are three basic types of space man experiences in nature: two-dimensional, three-dimensional, and four-dimensional.

Two-dimensional space *is that space created by the relationship of shape, line, texture, color and value. It exists on a surface and has length and breadth but lacks thickness and depth.*

Three-dimensional space *is actual space — that which exists in and around objects. It is distinguished from mass or objects.*

Two-dimensional space exists on this banana because of the relationship of a number of brown specks on a field of yellow. It exists in the specks themselves as well as in the yellow area on and around which the specks appear.

Three-dimensional space exists around both the banana and around the skull. However, the skull, due to its structure, is not as continuous a mass as the banana. Space may be said to flow through its various openings.

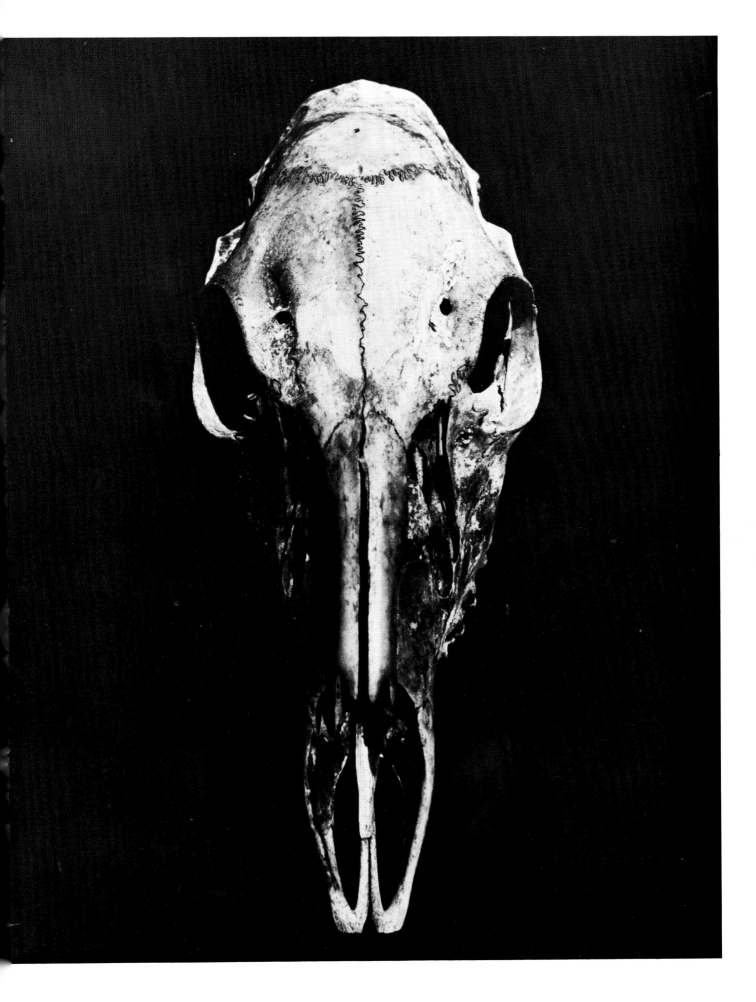

Three-dimensional space exists because of the nature of the universe. Man lives and moves within it. However, the character of three-dimensional space, as one experiences it, changes as the contours of the land and the objects occupying the space change.

The sense of three-dimensional space in this Illinois cornfield appears great because of the flatness of the land and the lack of objects in the foreground to break the continuity of the space.

Although the area photographed in this wood is as great as that in the cornfield, and although the land is as flat, the sense of space or spaciousness is not as overwhelming because the trees and the patterns of light and shadow act to break the continuity of the area.

Four dimensional space is space-time. A great part of one's visual experience includes objects or life in motion in four-dimensional space.

A comparison of three photographs of trees, one showing the group in a static condition, the others showing them moved by a strong wind, illustrates how the trees change in appearance when experienced in four-dimensional space.

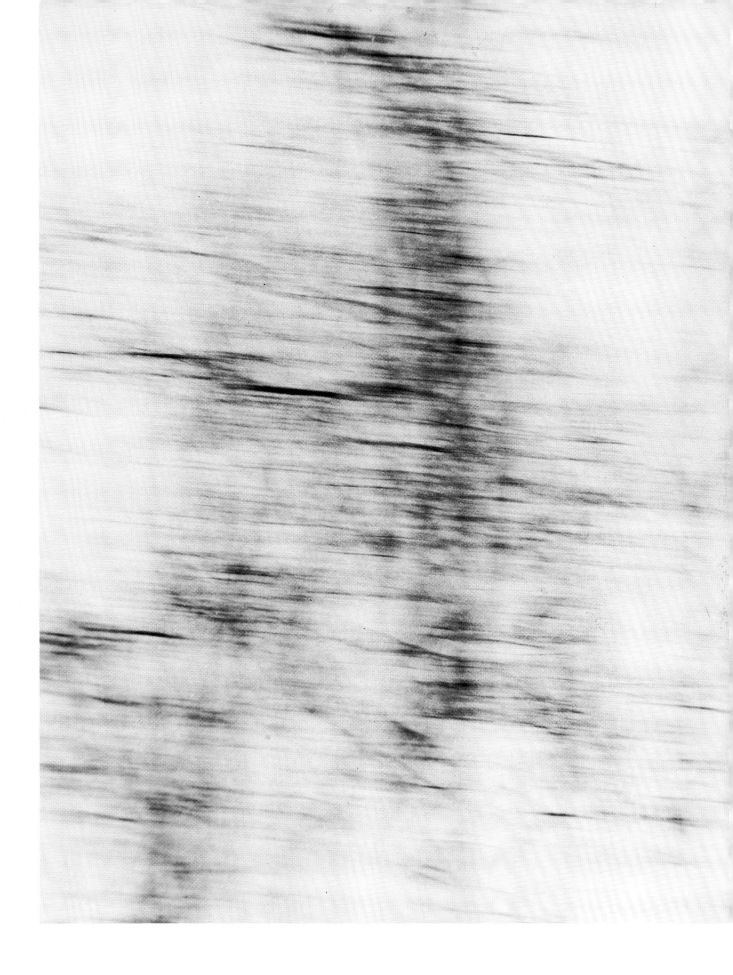

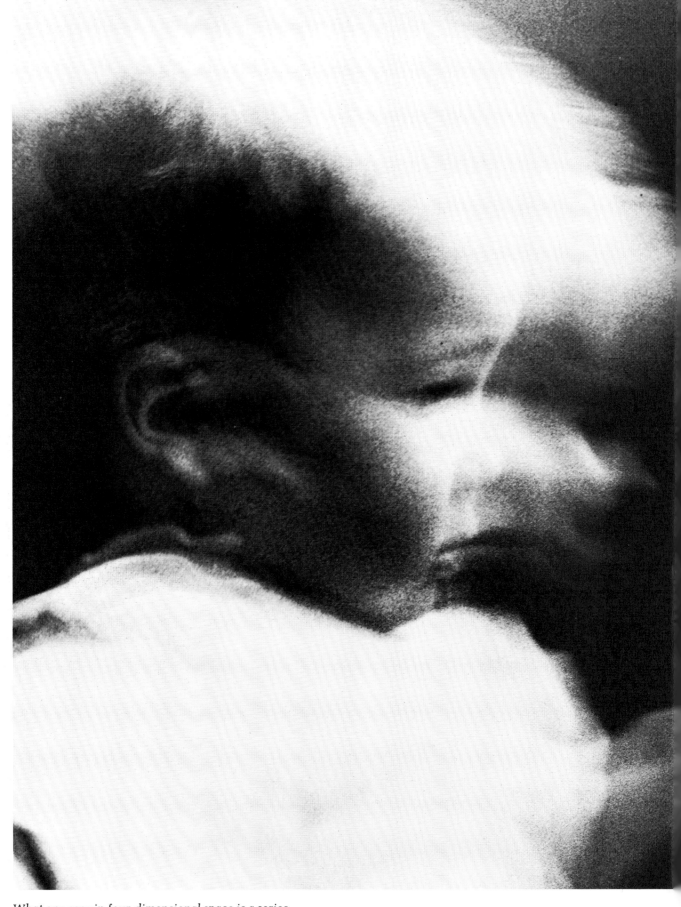

*What one sees in four-dimensional space is a series
of movements and a number of images. The camera
has recorded the young child and her movements
by a number of continuous blurred images.*

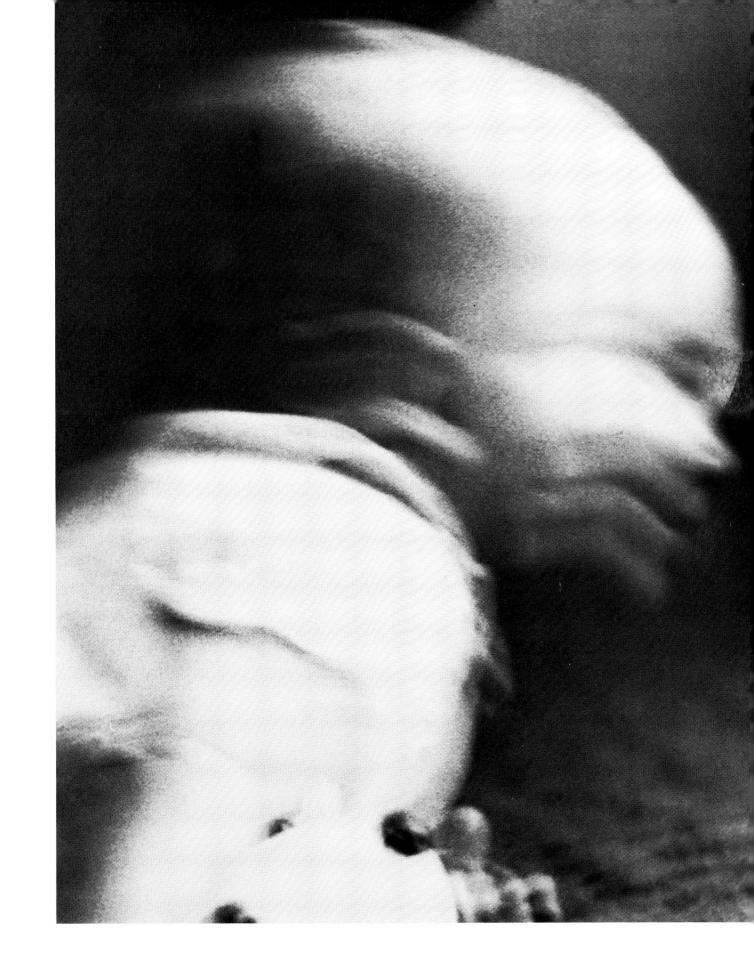

Physical laws govern how three-dimensional space is viewed and what happens to objects or areas within a particular field of vision.

Depending on their position, objects within a given spatial field will:

1. decrease in size and scale as they approach the horizon.

2. appear higher as the distance between the viewer and the horizon becomes greater.

3. appear less clear and lighter in value with greater distance, due to the construction of the human eye.

All three of these conditions are illustrated by the objects in the above photo. The size and relative scale of the trees decrease as the horizon is approached. The groups of trees are higher on the picture plane as their distance from the viewer increases, and the details of the trees are less clear and values lighter as the distance from the viewer increases.

All of these facts are further illustrated in this view by the edge of a beach. Compared with the piece of seaweed in the foreground, the figure in the background is relatively small, higher on the picture plane, lighter in value and less distinct.

Another indication of three-dimensional space is the overlapping of objects or areas or parts of objects or areas. If a part of the visible surface of one object or area is hidden by another, it is located in space farther away.

A familiar example of overlapping is found in groups of hills and mountains. As seen here, the closer hills hide part of those more distant.

The tree overlapping the water and the hill behind indicates to the viewer that the tree is closer to his position.

Another indication of three-dimensional space is the principle of linear perspective. If one looks out into space, objects decrease in relative size and rise relative to the viewer's position as they approach the horizon. If arranged along parallel lines, they also seem to converge to a point in space often called the "vanishing point".

Although actually parallel to each other, the rows of corn seem to converge at a point on the horizon. This illustrates the principle of linear perspective.

The tracks in the road are also parallel. However, they seem to converge as a certain point in space is approached.

Three-dimensional space is also revealed due to the nature of certain materials and the way light is projected and reflected. Although one object or area may lie behind another, it is possible to see both simultaneously if the material in front possesses a certain degree of transparency. Water, air, light, fruit, crystal, ice, wings of insects and flower petals are materials often possessing various degrees of transparency.

The most common example of transparency is air. In varying degrees, the coating of ice on the branches in photo at left reveal space because of the transparent nature of ice.

Although certain parts of the seaweed (below) are under water, they may be seen by the viewer, because water is transparent.

The apparent position of an object or area is determined in part by its value and by shadows. When a light source is located in front of an object or area, that which lies behind often receives cast shadows and appears darker in value than that in front.

Shadow helps to define the various positions in space of certain parts of the piece of wood at left.

The relative positions in space of certain parts of the mold at right are defined because of the shadows cast by those areas closest to the light.